MIDLAND FOX
A PICTORIAL HISTORY
1984–1997

ANDREW BARTLETT

First published 2026

Amberley Publishing
The Hill, Stroud
Gloucestershire, GL5 4EP

www.amberley-books.com

Copyright © Andrew Bartlett, 2026

The right of Andrew Bartlett to be identified as the Author of this work has been asserted in accordance with the Copyrights, Designs and Patents Act 1988.

ISBN 978 1 3981 2399 1 (print)
ISBN 978 1 3981 2400 4 (ebook)

All rights reserved. No part of this book may be reprinted or reproduced or utilised in any form or by any electronic, mechanical or other means, now known or hereafter invented, including photocopying and recording, or in any information storage or retrieval system, without the permission in writing from the Publishers.

British Library Cataloguing in Publication Data.
A catalogue record for this book is available from the British Library.

Origination by Amberley Publishing.
Printed in the UK.

Appointed GPSR EU Representative: Easy Access System Europe Oü, 16879218
Address: Mustamäe tee 50, 10621, Tallinn, Estonia
Contact Details: gpsr.requests@easproject.com, +358 40 500 3575

Contents

Introduction	4
The Midland Red East Inheritance	6
Midland Fox Takes to the Road	9
The Minibus Revolution	22
Privatisation and the Acquisition Trail	25
The British Bus and Cowie Group Years	73

Introduction

When the Midland Red empire was split up in September 1981, four bus-operating units were created, designated East, South, West and North. Midland Red East was the only one to drop the geographic identifier on its vehicles (though not on its timetables). It was also the first to break away from National Bus Company (NBC) corporate livery, using a deeper shade of red on repaints to the existing fleet and on former London Fleetlines first acquired in 1982. It should be noted that since the early 1970s, Midland Red policy had been to invest solely in single-decker buses and coaches, which disadvantaged Midland Red East given the urban nature of much of its operating area. By the end of 1983, even before the new company was born, over seventy new and second-hand double-deck buses had been acquired, with a further fourteen arriving in January 1984, replacing Midland Red-era Daimler Fleetlines and Leyland National saloons.

The search was also on for a fresh identity. A bright yellow and red livery was first seen towards the end of 1983, most notably on the new Leyland Olympians. After weeks of teasers in the local press, suggesting readers should 'Follow the Fox', Midland Fox took to the streets on Sunday 15 January 1984 – the formal launch came the following day. Leicestershire was the principal operating area, but longer-distance services took Midland Fox buses and coaches as far afield as Nottinghamshire, Derbyshire, the West Midlands and Warwickshire, Staffordshire, Northamptonshire and Cambridgeshire. The company's garages were based at Leicester (Southgate Street), Wigston (Station Street), Coalville (Ashby Road), Swadlincote (Midland Road) and Market Harborough (Springfield Street), with outstations at Alrewas, Barwell, Loughborough and Melton Mowbray.

The company's history over the next thirteen years shows it to have been one of the more innovative NBC subsidiaries as it prepared for deregulation and privatisation. Midland Fox management hit the ground running, and two key events from 1984/85 did much to immediately strengthen the company's position. In May 1984, an argument that had been ongoing for years was finally resolved in favour of Midland Fox. Leicester City Transport (LCT) had gained a significant advantage in the 1930s when the council placed restrictions on Midland Red's ability to pick up and set down passengers within Leicester's boundaries. With the provisions of the 1980 Transport Act on its side, Midland Fox took the issue to the Traffic Commissioners once more and won its case. The resulting increase in LCT and Midland Fox services combined on weekdays along the city's main arteries was over 100 per cent, although initially Midland Fox buses would call on average at one in every two stops.

Next, and following the successful trial of Ford Transit minibuses by Devon General in Exeter, similar plans were drawn up for Leicester, city and county. The result was one of the largest operations in the country at that time. 'Fox Cub' networks were rolled out between July 1985 and April 1986 in Coalville, Hinckley, Market Harborough, Ashby de la Zouch, Burton on Trent and Swadlincote. In Leicester itself, ten services, most of which provided new cross-city links, were introduced from September to December 1985. Although records of the Traffic Commissioners' proceedings show that Leicester CityBus (LCB), as it became in September 1984, was offered some form of joint operation, this was turned down, thus giving Midland Fox an even greater advantage in terms of market share. Sandacre Street garage, closed in 1980 and latterly used as an NCP car park, reopened in January 1986 as a base for the Fox Cub fleet.

The sale of NBC subsidiaries had begun in mid-1985, but it would be a further two years before Midland Fox left the fold. On 18 August 1987 it was sold to its managers (70 per cent) and Stevensons of Uttoxeter (30 per cent, which consisted of the garage at Swadlincote and some forty vehicles). For Midland Fox, this marked the start of a three-year buying spree:

- in 1988, Wreake Valley Travel (January), Heeps (Premier Coaches) (February), Fairtax Foxhound (April), Bates (Reg's Coaches) (July), Astill and Jordan, and County Travel's contracts and vehicles only, both in October.
- in 1989, Shelton Orsborn (April), Loughborough Coach & Bus Company (LC&B) (May) and G K Kinch (commercial bus operations and vehicles, in October). One condition of the Kinch acquisition, which ended a bus war on the Loughborough corridor, was that this would not compete in Leicestershire for the next three years.
- in 1990, NWP Travel (April), Tellings Golden Miller (TGM) (June) and Blands of Stamford (July).
- in 1991, TGM acquired both V & M Hills and The Coach Travel Centre in January and Sheenway Coaches in March.

Some of these companies were purely coaching concerns. Midland Fox had always participated in National Express services and run touring programmes, but these latter aspects of the business assumed greater importance following the Fairtax acquisition and the adoption of the Foxhound name.

The late 1980s had seen the emergence of new bus company groups: Stagecoach, Badgerline and Drawlane. Midland Fox joined Drawlane on 4 September 1989, which was renamed British Bus in November 1992.

After setting up the 177-strong minibus fleet, vehicle purchasing policy in subsequent years tended in the main towards second-hand stock, although there were some notable acquisitions of new buses and coaches.

The decision to sell LCB in 1993 sparked one final bus war, instituted by Midland Fox, which registered services to Goodwood, Rushey Mead, Evington, the Beaumont Centre and Mowmacre Hill in the city, and Newbold Verdon in the county, running in direct opposition to LCB in the hope that it would detract potential bidders. LCB responded with routes to Syston and Queniborough, Groby and Ratby, Loughborough, Wigston and Hinckley. Inevitably, both sides discovered that the competing services were not economically viable, and after a bid from Grampian Regional Transport for LCB was accepted, a more harmonious co-existence followed.

In September 1995, the garage at Sandacre Street closed for the final time, with its vehicles transferred to a new site on Westmoreland Avenue in Thurmaston.

In 1996 British Bus was sold to the Cowie Group. The end of the Midland Fox era came a year later when the bus operations were renamed Arriva. An aquamarine and stone livery was introduced, and vehicles now promoted the new name plus a 'local' byline, which in the case of Leicestershire read 'Arriva serving the Fox County'. In my view, this forfeited the immediacy and the marketing potential of the Midland Fox name.

A few author's notes to finish with. All the photographs were either taken by me or are from my collection. Locations of photos in Leicester are identified by the road name only, or in the case of the main terminal, St Margaret's. To continually repeat 'Leicester' or 'bus station' seemed unnecessary to me – so I haven't. On the other hand, locations outside the city boundary are fully described.

The Midland Red East Inheritance

Among the changes planned by Midland Red East managers was a new livery, but this version, in yellow and red, did not find favour and it became an advertisement for return tickets (offside) and season tickets (nearside) instead. Fresh from the paint shop, Alexander-bodied Daimler Fleetline 6117 (LHA 617F) was being admired in St Margaret's.

Midland Red's first fifty-two Leyland Leopards with dual-purpose seating were bodied by Willowbrook; seven came to Midland Red East, including 6412 (YHA 412J), pictured in Wetmore Park bus station, Burton on Trent. Coalville was the only Leicestershire garage to adopt a MAP (Market Analysis Project) local identity – Lancer. MAP was based on the principle that garages should be able to support themselves financially but was never implemented in Leicester or Wigston and its use was quietly phased out by Midland Red East.

Half the coaching fleet was drawn from the 1980 intake, some of which were for National Express services while the remainder were to grant specification and could be used on stage carriage routes. With that in mind, Leyland Leopard/Willowbrook 800 (BVP 800V) was given 'Expressway' livery and was awaiting its next turn on the X66 to Birmingham in St Margaret's.

London Transport's decision to begin offloading Daimler Fleetlines was a godsend to Midland Red East, and seventy-seven joined the fleet between 1982 and 1984. A May 1982 arrival, 2801 (GHM 801N) was allocated to Wigston and seen in St Margaret's later that year. Most of those coming to Midland Red East were bodied by Metro-Cammell. A change to the livery saw a deeper shade of red adopted.

Former National Travel Willowbrook-bodied Leyland Leopards with fleet numbers 50–57 entered service in May/June 1983, working out of either Southgate Street, Wigston or Coalville. 52 (XCW 152R) was awaiting its next X67 duty to Coventry while Marshall-bodied Leopard 206 was arriving for a turn on the 174 to Coalville. This St Margaret's view dates from October 1983.

Always a Southgate Street bus, 712 (TOF 712S) was one of the first vehicles to adopt the new yellow and red livery, and was engaged on a Thurcaston working at St Margaret's on 12 October 1983. Leyland National fleet numbers had a '3' added in 1984, so this example would become 3712. It moved to Midland Red West and reverted to its old number in 1986.

The first seven of twelve new ECW-bodied Leyland Olympians entered service from Southgate Street in October 1983 and had yellow and red livery from the outset. Parked up in St Margaret's during that month, the next duty for 4504 (A504 EJF) will be a run on the 628 to Loughborough and Shepshed.

Midland Fox Takes to the Road

Midland Red had two batches of Alexander-bodied Daimler Fleetlines, classified DD12 and DD13. Midland Fox inherited four DD12s, the oldest of which lasted into the summer of 1985. There were twenty-one DD13s, including 6195 (UHA 195H), seen in Belgrave Gate in August 1984 on the recently introduced 94A Groby/Ratby circular. It lasted a further two years before withdrawal.

The final batch of DD13s had a redesigned front panel so were easy to spot. Wigston-based 6277 (YHA 277J) was one of the few repainted into Midland Fox livery. Seen in Charles Street, it was on its way to Broughton Astley on the 84 in 1985, the year it was withdrawn.

The seven dual-purpose-bodied Leyland Leopards had been reduced to three by January 1984. Returning from Oadby alongside Victoria Park in 1984, 6422 (CHA 422K) was a rare visitor to the principal London Road route.

When the first batch of fifty-eight Leyland Nationals arrived in 1972/73, Midland Red started a new numbering system. The first, 101, worked out of both Leicester garages until a move to Wigston in May 1980. Renumbered 3101 (HHA 101L), it was photographed in 1984 in High Street on the short-lived express X32 service to Hinckley via the M69 motorway. It went to Midland Red West in early 1985, and was secured for preservation in 2008.

Marshall dual-purpose-bodied Leyland Leopards came in two batches of fifty each, classified S27 and S28, between 1973 and 1975. Midland Red East had almost equal numbers of both types. A long-serving S28, 354 (GOH 354N), moved to Coalville garage in 1978 and stayed there for seventeen years. Ashby Road, Coalville, was the location when in April 1993 it was en route to Swadlincote on the 118.

The Midland Express name was carried on vehicles from all four Midland Red companies that were used on longer-distance stage carriage routes. Midland Red East painted several coaches and dual-purpose vehicles in the scheme, including 365 (GOL 365N), which was loaned by Midland Red South for six months in 1982 before the transfer was made permanent. It was working the limited stop X67 service, which linked Leicester with Coventry, Warwick, where the photo was taken, and Stratford-upon-Avon.

A number of coaches based in Leicester at the time Midland Red East was formed were under the control of Midland Red Express, but responsibility was transferred early in 1982, along with Plaxton-bodied Leyland Leopards 195, 449, 611, 779/80. National Express-liveried 780 (BVP 780V) was loading in Loughborough for a 430 service to London during 1984.

The first six former London Transport Daimler Fleetlines arrived in Leicester within four months of Midland Red East's formation. One was 2739 (SMU 739N), pictured alongside one of the concrete shelters at St Margaret's. Dating from 1941, when the facility first opened, they were now very much showing their age.

New to Cumberland in 1974, Leyland Leopard 2610 (VYM 505M) was acquired by Midland Red East in April 1982 and thereafter spent most of its time at Wigston. After spells in National Express and Midland Express livery, my photo is from the end of its career when it was sent to Market Harborough. On a grey 8 June 1991 it was awaiting the next duty on the local villages service in the bus station.

Above and below: Midland Red East introduced the 'Night Bus' concept in November 1983 with five new services on Friday and Saturday nights along key corridors out of the city at midnight, 1.00 a.m. and 2.00 a.m. Only 2781 (GHM 781N), seen in St Margaret's in February 1984 on a daytime run to Queniborough, received the special livery. The 'Night Bus' routes were not successful and were withdrawn by May 1984, when 2781 received overall advertising for Y-Fronts. High Street is the location; at this time, the 74 was a cross-town service between Braunstone and Beaumont Leys.

Another 1982 arrival from London, 2778 (GHM 778N) was pictured in St Nicholas Circle on the 7 South Wigston and Wigston Magna circular in the early days of Midland Fox ownership. At the outset, the company had merged Wigston and Birstall services to provide a new cross-town link, but timekeeping was adversely affected by congestion and the idea was later dropped.

A new Leyland Tiger/Plaxton coach in National Holidays livery arrived in May 1983, appropriately receiving fleet number 1 (BRY 1Y). It was parked up in Southgates on 5 May 1985, six months before it was re-registered URH 657. Once its front-line coaching days were over (June 1988), it moved to Wigston and was often found on the Market Harborough route.

The first of three photos depicting second-hand Leyland Leopard/Plaxton acquisitions. One of three that arrived in May 1984 from National Travel (London) when just three years old, 612 (NMV 612W) had a varied career as a front-line coach, part of the short-lived Fen Travel operation and later, the only vehicle to receive blue 'Training Fox' livery. It was seen in Burleys Way in 1984; the blue boards mask the rebuilding work at St Margaret's.

New to Evans, Bedminster, 71 (HHW 471X) came to Midland Red East in July 1983. Seen at St Margaret's in May 1984, it had received dual-purpose livery and in N & S Coaches style had been named *Kathryn*.

Leyland Leopard 784 (BVP 784V) was a former Midland Red West vehicle that moved to Coalville garage at the end of 1981. Three years later it was preparing to turn into Nottingham's Victoria Centre bus and coach station with an X99 working. The path of the old Great Central Railway and the (blocked off) entrance to the Woodborough Road tunnel could be clearly seen on the other side of the concrete wall.

Midland Red classified its Leyland Nationals in the series N1 to N9, and Midland Red East inherited some of all bar the N2s and N9s. The one with the highest fleet number was N8 716; this is the second highest, 715, now 3715 (TOF 715S), leaving St Margaret's for Groby in the mid-1980s.

The first eleven of the new Leyland Olympians settled at Southgate Street, while 4512 was despatched to Coalville. They were often found on the Loughborough corridor, and demonstrating the many promotional uses to which the Fox name was put, for some years 4507 (A507 EJF) carried the name *Foxtrotter* above the front wheel arches. It also happened to be the name of the 'Day Out By Bus' ticket.

The sale of N & S Coaches of Market Harborough to Midland Red East was completed on Christmas Day 1983, and included the garage on Springfield Street. Seven Ford R1114/Plaxton coaches and a single Plaxton-bodied DAF MB200 were acquired, and one of the Fords, now 7006 *Pauline* (EUT 10T), is seen looking particularly smart in Foxhound livery but with Midland Fox fleetnames, tucked away inside Southgate Street garage on 29 October 1986. The Fords lasted up to seven years with Midland Fox, and were all sold on for further service.

London Transport DMS1535 went to Western National (828) before arriving at Swadlincote in January 1984, where it was pressed into service wearing green Cornwall Busways livery. Numbered 2705 (THM 535M) and seen in Station Street, Burton upon Trent, it went to the paint shop after transfer to Southgate Street in August, receiving overall advertising for British Telecom.

All six ex-Western National Daimler Fleetlines spent some time at Swadlincote in their first year in the Midlands. Another recipient of advertising livery was 2715 (TGX 859M), which wore this design for the Leicester Trader freesheet for over four years. In this 1985 photo it was approaching the Clock Tower on the cross-town 4 (Wigston Magna–East Goscote).

Ten ECW-bodied Leyland Fleetlines, new to Yorkshire Woollen in 1972, arrived at the end of 1984. Almost as old as the vehicle it was replacing, 2623 (LHD 312K) was on its way to Wigston in May 1985, followed by an LCB Dennis Dominator six years its junior. Some claimed Midland Fox yellow could be mistaken for LCB cream, so the council introduced a diamond containing the city crest between decks, but this was later changed to the style shown on the Dominator.

A strange choice for overall advertising, but nonetheless April 1987 saw sister vehicle 2619 (LHD 308K) given this interesting scheme for Children's World at Boots, which it retained until its withdrawal at the end of 1988. It was departing St Margaret's that year for Hinckley and Nuneaton, not that the blind is any help to would-be passengers.

Two more Leyland Olympians came to Southgate Street in October and December 1984 respectively. The second of these, 4514 (B514 LFP), received the Eagle Star offside advertisement from new. It was parked up at the entrance to St Margaret's in 1985; later in life it was converted to open-top format for the 'Discover Leicester' sightseeing tour.

Making the journey south from West Riding in April 1985, four Alexander-bodied Leyland Leopards were not taken into stock immediately, hence the Yorkshire fleet name and 'On Hire' notice on West Riding 2 (HWY 718N). It became Midland Fox 370, and with 371/75/80, was assigned to Swadlincote. All four passed to Stevensons as part of the management buyout.

More second-hand Leyland Leopards joined the fleet around this time. Ex-National Travel (North West) 470/75 had come via Ribble in 1984, while 620/24 moved from National Travel (South West) to Black & White in June 1984 and a year later were leased to Midland Fox, an arrangement that lasted until October 1987 when both went to dealers. This is 624 (DDG 260T) at Surrey Street bus station, Norwich, in 1986.

The former 5828 (GHA 328D) was one of two Midland Red LC9 Leyland Leopard/Plaxton coaches converted for towing duties in 1978. Midland Red East numbered it 9000 in 1981; the other vehicle, 9001 (ex-5831, GHA 331D, a 1980 conversion) was assigned to Wigston. Both saw twenty years' service before withdrawal, which came in Arriva days; this Southgate Street garage photo is from May 1986.

Photographed in the Southgate Street garage yard in August 1984, Leyland Titan PD2/MCW 9010 (HBF 679D) was new as Harper Brothers 27, becoming Midland Red 2227 and passing to Midland Red East as a trainer in September 1981. Withdrawn in April 1991, it is now with the Transport Museum at Wythall.

The Minibus Revolution

Ford Transit minibuses had been introduced successfully in Exeter during 1984 and Midland Fox management made plans for networks in both city and county. The fleetname settled upon was Fox Cub, an inspired choice that ensured strong brand recognition. The roll-out began in Coalville on 27 July 1985, and Rootes-bodied M1 (B401 NJF) was photographed inside the garage there. It was saved for preservation after withdrawal in 1992.

Such was the urgency to introduce the new services that a batch of thirty, bodied this time by Robin Hood, were diverted from Bristol; only M25 kept its original registration of B400 WTC. M28 (B428 PJF) was seen in Southgate Street garage yard on 7 August 1985, not as yet kitted out for service. The first phase of the city network roll-out began on 21 September 1985, with the second the following month and the third in December.

Eight days after the introduction in Leicester, Fox Cubs M15-24 started work in Hinckley. After just over a year, this original batch moved on, all except two appearing at the newly reopened Sandacre Street garage. Nine years later and Transits still had a presence in the town, with M108 (C508 TJF) in Altus advertising livery at rest at the Jacknall Road premises in June 1994.

Only one further network was introduced in 1985. On 7 December, Fox Cubs began work in Market Harborough with a cross-town route and a country service to The Langtons, Kibworth and Fleckney. M95 (C495 TBC) was bodied by Dormobile, and demonstrates how useful the Transits were in terms of overall advertising. The location is the old Market Harborough bus station, which was redeveloped in the early 1990s.

A fourth body builder was Alexander, which supplied seventeen Transits, M98 to M114. With a 'Quick Stitch' overall advertisement, M98 (C498 TJF) was crossing from Humberstone Gate to Charles Street in 1988, followed by a brand-new LCB Iveco. When in 1986 the popularity of the Fox Cubs was front-page news, the Transport Committee chair maintained that LCB would not use minibuses. In the end, financial constraints brought about in part by the Fox Cubs' success made it inevitable.

The last three Fox Cub networks were introduced in 1986, serving Ashby de la Zouch (March), Burton on Trent and Swadlincote (both April). M3 (B403 NJF), always a Coalville vehicle, was working an Ashby town service in Market Street in April 1992.

Privatisation and the Acquisition Trail

After all the Transits had arrived there were no further bus purchases in 1986, but National Express work was big business for Midland Fox and in April five new MCW Metroliners were acquired for the London service, taking fleet numbers 7050–54. Spotted in Buckingham Palace Road, SW1, early in its career, 7050 (C50 VJU) lasted until November 1992 and then went to Cheshire for use as a promotional vehicle for car cleaning products.

The twelve Leyland Leopards new to Midland Red Express in June 1982 were dispersed to the regional companies in November 1986, Midland Fox taking seven. This is Willowbrook-bodied 839 (LOA 839X), in receipt of up-to-date Foxhound livery, parked up in Southgates on a misty Sunday morning, 4 October 1987.

Competition from Gilbert Kinch on the Loughborough corridor in late 1986 prompted retaliation from Midland Fox. Two Leyland Nationals were given a revised livery and Midland Wolf fleetnames. Heavily promoting the cheap fares on offer, 3641 (PUK 641R) was awaiting its next duty on the X25 in Loughborough bus station.

Deregulation had seen Stevenson's build up a portfolio of routes in Birmingham, and after the buyout, the former Midland Fox Leyland National 3416 (GOL 416N) was employed on one such working between Sutton Coldfield and Erdington – though the blind displays still hark back to its days in Coalville. After just two months it was sold on.

Among the Ford Transits to join Stevenson's were the last five numerically in the Midland Fox fleet, all of which were former Sandacre Street vehicles. Dormobile-bodied M174 (C574 TUT) became plain 174, and apart from the legal lettering, there are few other signs of the changed ownership in this photo from the winter of 1987/88.

Autumn 1987 saw the arrival of three more Ford R1114s. Plaxton-bodied 7010 came from Fowler of Holbeach Drove, while 7011/12 were Duple-bodied examples from Bebb, Nantwit Fadre. They were allocated to Market Harborough and lasted until February 1990. On 28 September 1988 7011 (NDW 39X) was seen in Kettering bus station; Midland Fox had since deregulation encroached into United Counties territory.

Midland Fox broke new ground when acquiring two second-hand Bristol VR3s new to Devon General, 1112/13, in late 1987; twelve more from three other operators followed in 1988. They spent the next five years in Leicester, and many, including 1113 (VDV 113S), then found a new home with Crosville Wales. On this occasion, however, it was working a 43 service to Wigston Magna.

Wreake Valley Travel was the first company acquired by Midland Fox, the deal taking place in January 1988. Three Leyland Nationals and two Northern Counties-bodied Daimler Fleetlines, all previously with Greater Manchester Buses, were included in the sale, along with three coaches. This is Fleetline 4 (VNB 227L), seen in St Margaret's prior to the takeover. Midland Fox used fleet numbers in the range from 9200 on paper for acquired vehicles whose futures might be described as short-term, thus 4 became 9203.

Midland Fox kept the Wreake Valley name alive and built up numbers through transfers from both the main fleet and other acquired companies. Leyland National 3142 (NPD 142L) was a former Kinch vehicle which became Wreake Valley 16. Photographed in Humberstone Gate in August 1990, it was about to work a shortened version of the 10 which competed with Leicester CityBus. Withdrawn in January 1992, it resurfaced in August 1994 as Greenway conversion 2157.

The three ex-Wreake Valley coaches comprised two Plaxton-bodied Bedfords of 1986 vintage and the year older Bova EL28/Duple, 8007 (B196 PAY). In plain white livery and with Foxhound fleetnames, it was hemmed in outside the Alexandra Hotel on King Edward's Parade, Eastbourne, in 1988. It was re-registered LJI 5632 the following year.

One of the two Midland Wolf Leyland Nationals was pictured earlier. This is the other one, 3491 (JOX 491P), resting in St Margaret's on 9 April 1988. Both regained Midland Fox fleetnames in late 1987 when transferred to Wigston, but were back in Loughborough again in May 1989 when LC&B operations were acquired.

Midland Fox favoured Carlyle-bodied Iveco 49.10s for the next generation of minibuses, and the initial batch, M201–18, came in February 1988. Most carried overall advertising at some point in their lives, in the case of M204 (E204 HRY) only months after its arrival. Pictured in Humberstone Gate en route to Eyres Monsel, it appears much more robust than its Ford Transit cousin M39, seen alongside.

The first MCW Metrobuses to join the fleet were four ex-South Yorkshire PTE examples which came via Stevensons, acting as a dealer in this instance. The quartet, 2474/84/88/91, entered service in March 1988. Looking as though it had come fresh from the paint shop, 2491 (EWF 491V) had just returned from Oadby in this Belgrave Gate scene on 20 August 1988.

Iveco 49.10s M219/20 also appeared in March 1988 and even with dual-purpose seating still catered for twenty-five passengers. Based at Wigston, they were often found on the X49, which served a new housing estate at Wigston Harcourt. Returning from there, M219 (E519 TOV) was crossing the Charles Street/Humberstone Gate junction, overtaking Leicester Citybus Dennis Dominator 85, which was employed on Tesco contract work.

Midland Fox acquired the business of John Penniston trading as **Fairtax Foxhound** on 1 April 1988. The mixed fleet included Volvo, Bedford, Leyland Leopard, Mercedes and AEC Reliance coaches, along with four minibuses. The Mercedes O303/Jonckheere, 14 (XLC 1S, B514 CBD), new in May 1985, was a high-profile member of the coaching holiday fleet. Seen at the Burton Street, Melton Mowbray, garage on 3 November 1993, it had reverted back to Penniston ownership a few months earlier but was sold in May 1994.

New to Glyn, Mossley, Fairtax acquired this Fiat 60F10/Caetano in September 1987 and after the Midland Fox takeover it took fleet number M455 (BND 955Y). The photo was taken at the Burton Street garage in 1989; despite looking somewhat abandoned at the time, it was repainted and soldiered on until June 1995.

Ford-bodied Transit M466 (E955 LNR, NEL 1F, E707 ERY) was new to Fairtax seven months before the takeover. With dual-purpose seating for twelve, it may have been found initially on local services, but in later life it was more likely to be used as staff transport. It had ventured to Leicester in 1993 and was parked up in the National Express bay outside St Margaret's.

Formerly with Cambus and new to Grey-Green, three Leyland Leopards with Duple Dominant bodywork were acquired in the same month as the Penniston takeover. They were put to work on an upgraded Leicester–Melton X1 service in plain biscuit brown livery with Fairtax fleetnames and Leicester Line logos, as seen on 362 (VYU 762S) in Burton Street, Melton Mowbray, on 20 August 1988.

At the same time, Melton Mowbray town services were recast and five consecutively numbered Ford Transits from Sandacre Street garage were transferred to work them. M81–85 were painted in Fairtax biscuit brown livery with a black skirt, and christened 'Melton Minis'. M82 (C482 TAY) was spotted in Leicester Street on route 3 to Tamar Road, also on 20 August 1988.

The early 1980s saw Leicester CityBus join forces with **County Travel**, building up a group of routes between Loughborough, Leicester and Fleckney numbered 121–24 in competition with Midland Fox. This came to an abrupt end in October 1988, when Midland Fox took over County Travel contracts and vehicles – two Leyland Leopards and five Daimler Fleetlines, all of which were immediately withdrawn. The photo is of MCW Metropolitan KJD 278P, one of several operated up to 1987, when they were sold in favour of the Fleetlines.

One of the last Bristol VR3s to come to Midland Fox was 1129 (YBW 605R), which, along with a couple of others, was initially put to work on County Travel contracts. Eighteen months later, it was employed on school service S46, which served Lutterworth College, and was seen turning into Bitteswell Road in the town.

Two final VR3s, 1149/50, were originally with Stevensons and 1149 (UVT 49X) was the last of the line. It was taking a break from duties on the 184 Dunton Bassett service when photographed on the parking area adjacent to the old weighbridge on Humberstone Gate. It was withdrawn in August 1992 and transferred to Crosville Wales.

New to Wallace Arnold, Plaxton-bodied Leyland Leopard 359 (HWU 59N) was one of a handful of vehicles that passed to Midland Fox following the acquisition of **Astill & Jordan** in October 1988. It lost their attractive blue and cream livery for this version of the Wreake Valley scheme, in whose fleet it was numbered 2. In this Charles Street photo from 1989, at least it is working the route long associated with Astill and Jordan.

In fact seven Astill & Jordan vehicles changed hands, of which only one Leyland Leopard and three ex-London Fleetlines saw more than a year's further service. Replacements for the others included 3350 (GHB 689N), a Leyland National new to Red & White in 1975 but received from National Welsh. It entered service in February 1990 in the blue and cream livery associated with Astill & Jordan, though numbered 11 in the Wreake Valley series.

Moving from National Express/National Holidays work to the touring fleet, Leyland Tiger coach 1 (URH 657, BRY 1Y) looked like a winner in the silver and black Foxhound livery. Most appropriate really, as it was photographed in Epsom on Derby Day, 1 June 1988.

In the final analysis, sixty-four Daimler/Leyland Fleetlines came directly from London in 1982 and 1983, plus another thirteen that worked with London Country or Western National before coming to Leicester. Entering service in 1983, 2734 (SMU 734N) was always a Southgate Street vehicle, and looked quite smart when seen in Leicester Road, Narborough, on 6 August 1988.

The twenty Leyland National 2s Midland Red had in the first half of 1980 were the last service buses received before the split. Of the eight that passed to Midland Fox, only 3827 had gone – to Stevensons – by the start of 1988. In August that year 3822 (BVP 822V) was in Charles Street on the Halls of Residence service 80A. I have a note that says it was the only bus working the 80 that day with correct blinds.

One of the two Leyland Tiger/Plaxton coaches new to London Country North East that came to Midland Fox in March 1989, 9 (A125 EPA) spent ten years at Wigston garage and was a regular on its longer-distance stage carriage services. On this occasion, however, it was deputising on National Express 440 to London as it departed Lincoln bus station.

A further twenty of the Iveco-badged twenty-five seaters, M221–40, were taken into stock between March and August 1989. Four of the first five had dual-purpose seating and M224/25 also received Foxhound livery. Seen in Humberstone Gate, M224 (F24 XVP) later carried this yellow and black scheme to advertise the Saturday Park & Ride sites operated by Midland Fox.

April 1989 saw the acquisition of **Shelton Orsborn** of Wollaston, Northamptonshire. Fourteen Leyland Leopards and DAF MB200s joined Midland Fox, taking fleet numbers between 65 and 88. One of the oldest Leopards, 75 (YCF 826, JNK 550N), was photographed whilst crossing the humpbacked bridge over the Grand Union Canal in Foxton. Having the route details on a board in the windscreen was not ideal.

New in August 1984, DAF MB200/Van Hool Alizee 87 (LJI 8157, B310 LUT) previously wore a two-tone blue and white Foxhound livery with Ambassador Royale fleet names and logos, the branding adopted in 1990 for group coaching holidays. But by December 1995 it was an ordinary member of the Foxhound fleet. At work in Market Harborough High Street, it had replaced the more usual dedicated Mercedes 709D on the Marks & Spencer shuttle service to Fosse Park, with greater passenger numbers expected for the post-Christmas sales.

Loughborough Coach & Bus (LC&B) was a unit set up by Leicester CityBus in 1987 to run minibuses known as 'Trippits' in the town. Included in the sale was the former Trent garage on Derby Road. In May 1989, LC&B was sold to Midland Fox and the Optare City Pacers 844–858 had the M-prefix added to their fleet numbers. They lasted three months; in August they went to Derby City Transport. The photo shows 849 (D849 CRY) at work in Loughborough prior to the sale.

Midland Fox drafted bigger buses of its own into Loughborough from the outset. Leyland National 3490 (JOX 490P) had spent eleven years at Coalville, but was painted into the green LC&B livery and put into service in May 1989; this High Street scene was captured on the 26th.

Above and below: Having taken over the LC&B operations, Midland Fox wanted to finally deal with the competition on the Leicester–Loughborough corridor, and so Green Bus was formed. Ten ex-Crosville Wales Leyland Olympians, 4490–94 and 4515–19, were received in May 1989; they operated in Crosville livery without fleetnames and with cheap fares on offer. In these two photos from May 1989, 4492 (MTU 118Y) is seen leaving St Margaret's, while 4515 (A131 SMA) waits at Loughborough bus station. Once hostilities ceased, all ten Olympians transferred to Wigston, but 4515 had a shorter life than the others, being withdrawn after accident damage in March 1993.

One of the former Kinch Leyland Nationals soon joined the LC&B fleet. Unlike the other recently acquired subsidiaries, vehicles deployed at Loughborough were numbered in the Midland Fox range, this example becoming 3201 (BCD 808L). It was loading for the 30-mile journey to Derby in Charles Street on 18 August 1990.

It wasn't just Leyland Nationals in the LC&B fleet. Leyland Leopards 841/44 worked for the subsidiary for eighteen months, both gaining green livery and 841 (LOA 841X) the Green Bus fleetname. It was parked up ahead of 844 in this Loughborough view from September 1989.

Three former Kinch Leyland Fleetlines, 2948/52/57, entered service with Midland Fox at Southgate Street garage in October 1989. The photo of Metro Cammell-bodied 2952 (SDA 502S) in Eastgates demonstrates the perils of trying for a working picture in a busy shopping environment.

One of three Leyland Olympians with East Lancs bodywork new to G & G of Royal Leamington Spa, 4520 (C30 EUH) was taken into stock in June 1989, its seventy-eight coach seats a boon to passengers on longer stage carriage services. It was leaving Greyfriars bus station in Northampton for Leicester in 1992, pictured alongside one of Northampton Transport's distinctive Alexander-bodied Bristol VR3s.

There was only one new Iveco minibus during 1989, M242 (F242 SJU), which was despatched to Hinckley outstation and stayed until withdrawal in 1997. Pictured in Regent Street on a local service to Burbage, it carried an overall advertisement for VW dealers Ashby & Mann for several years.

The first Mercedes midibuses for Midland Fox were two Robin Hood-bodied 709Ds, which went to Coalville garage in June 1989. At twenty-seven, they seated two more than the Ivecos, indicating where the third generation of smaller vehicles might come from. M301 (F301 RUT) was at the town's Memorial Square on 28 April 1993, along with Transit M121, working local services 11 and 12 respectively.

Vehicle transfers from Midland Fox to Wreake Valley were numerous, but 3450 (KDW 335P) went straight into the subsidiary fleet when received. It was new to Western Welsh in 1976 and was one of four Leyland Nationals acquired from National Welsh in August 1989. It was later transferred to Loughborough, but was withdrawn after accident damage in June 1993.

In November 1989, two months after joining the Drawlane group, Midland Fox received its first new double-deckers since 1983/84. Five Alexander-bodied Leyland Olympians were allocated to Wigston, and 4521 (G521 WJF) was on its way back to Leicester when seen in Blaby Road, South Wigston, in February 1990. They lasted until 1999, when they were sent to Arriva North West in exchange for Scania N113s of equivalent age.

After a year working out of Wigston and Market Harborough garages, Bristol VR3 1105 (AUD 461R) was transferred to Melton Mowbray in October 1989 and given this attractive version of the Fairtax livery. In 1992 it moved again, to the Fen Travel operation at Stamford, and was replaced by a Leyland Fleetline.

Too old for front-line coach work at thirteen, Leyland Leopard 461 (JOX 461P) was despatched to Coalville where it was a useful addition to the roster for the 99 service to Nottingham, on which duty it was photographed in the city's Canal Street. Upon withdrawal in 1994, it passed briefly to Crosville Wales, and then to Northern Bus of Anston.

Above and below: During the summer of 1988, interesting livery experiments were carried out on a couple of Leyland Leopards. Both 800 and 805 arrived at Wigston early in 1988 but 800 (BVP 800V) moved to Coalville a year later where it remained until withdrawal in 1994; the photo was taken in Swadlincote bus station in 1989. 805 (BVP 805V) remained at either Wigston or Market Harborough until 1993; this photo was taken in St Margaret's, also in 1989. Neither style found favour, and repainting into fleet livery ensued.

Above and below: Two late 1980s photographs of rail replacement services for the Leicester–Birmingham line, possibly required because of problems at Arley tunnel, west of Nuneaton, which suffered from water ingress and mining subsidence. First, 2914 (KJD 9P), pictured leaving Nuneaton rail station, one of the last seven Fleetlines amassed by Midland Red East that were badged as Leylands. West Midlands Travel was also involved, and in this scene outside Leicester station, their MCW Metrobus 2667 is being passed by an almost empty Midland Fox Ford Transit, M68 (C468 TAY), with its rather tatty homemade destination information.

Most of the C21 class of Plaxton-bodied Leyland Leopards had by now received either Foxhound or Leicester Line livery, and were still active on stage carriage and holiday or tours work. Indeed, 779 (BVP 779V) had taken to the sea in May 1989, but only across the Solent as far as the Isle of Wight. It was seen in Bembridge.

Another Fairtax livery variant could be found on Leyland Tiger/Plaxton 7 (ANA 109Y), seen outside Burton Street garage, Melton Mowbray, in this early morning photo from July 1991. Received in February 1990, Fairtax was the sixth fleetname it had carried to date, following National Travel (West), Ribble, North Western, London Country South West and Speedlink Motor Services.

In fact, London & Country (the renamed London Country South West) supplied a further eleven Leyland Tiger coaches in 1990, with bodywork by Berkhof, Roe (all sold on within the year), Duple and Plaxton. The three Plaxton-bodied examples, 19–21, served well into the 2000s, with 19 (109 CRC, A103 HNC) the longest of all. It was seen at Southgates in May 1993, its fleetnames having gone missing.

Three of the Duple-bodied Tigers received in March 1990 began life with Shamrock & Rambler. After the loss of National Express contracts that led to its closure, they passed briefly to London Country (South West). While 28/29 went to Fairtax, 23 (BPR 103Y) spent most of its new life at Wigston, and was a regular on longer-distance work, such as in this North Street East, Uppingham, view of the X47 Leicester–Peterborough route.

Very much a one-off acquisition, Carlyle-bodied Ford Transit M183 (C603 NPU) came from Eastern National in March 1990. Unique is also the word that best describes its livery. It was immediately allocated to Market Harborough, and in this shot in the town's High Street, it is about to demonstrate how it will accommodate this sizeable queue in its twenty-seat body.

When the former Cambus Leyland Leopards were moved on to more mundane duties, DAF MB230/Plaxton 192/93 were two of the more modern vehicles acquired from Barton Buses of Chilwell for the Fairtax fleet in May 1990. This is 193 (C633 PAU) on the Melton Mowbray service in Syston Road, Queniborough, on 11 June 1994. It was withdrawn after accident damage in October 1997.

Above and below: Nottingham City Transport loaned ten Leyland National 2s in total during the period May to September 1990 while work in the Syston area precluded the use of double-deckers. With both carrying 'On hire to Midland Fox' notices in the destination screen, 706 (GTO 706V) was photographed in St Nicholas Circle on 18 August, while 709 (GTO 709V) was seen in Belgrave Gate on 13 June.

Three more Leyland Olympians from Crosville Cymru turned up in May 1990. Two were allocated to Southgate Street (4526/28) while Coalville had the third, 4527 (B187 BLG). Pictured outside Broadmarsh bus station, Nottingham, on 1 December 1992, it remained at Coalville until joining the Confidence, Leicester, fleet, along with 4528, in March 2008.

Tellings Golden Miller (TGM) of Byfleet, Surrey, joined the group in June 1990. The acquisition gave Midland Fox a foothold in the London area, providing an opportunity to bid for tendered services. Some TGM Volvo B10Ms transferred to Midland Fox and became regulars on the London service, such as 213 (FIL 3451, F803 TMD), sporting the registration recently given up by Leyland Tiger 3. It was collecting its London-bound passengers on the National Express stand at St Margaret's in 1995.

TGM had twelve Van Hool Alizee-bodied B10Ms in 1989. Carrying the smart white, yellow and blue fleet livery is 221 (F811 TMD), which on 15 May 1993 had brought its tour party to Huntingdon, and was parked up in Mill Common bus station while they explored the town.

TGM succeeded in winning the tenders for London Buses routes 116/117 in 1991 but operating them with ageing Leyland Nationals drawn from the Leicester fleets led to problems which were only overcome when the routes and vehicles were transferred to fellow Drawlane subsidiary London & Country in January 1992. Seen in High Street, Hounslow, 3562 (NOE 562R) displays TGM's attractive bus livery.

A visit to the TGM premises in Byfleet on 7 July 1992 found Ford Transit M102 (C502 TJF) on site, together with a Van Hool-bodied Volvo B10M and Toyota Coaster M275 (H275 GRY) – note the Leicester registration. TGM and all its subsidiaries left Midland Fox following a management buyout in July 1993.

Seemingly always in the market for good second-hand stock, Midland Fox invested in twenty-seven Alexander-bodied Leyland Fleetlines from South Yorkshire Transport in June 1990, which were split more or less equally between Southgate Street and Wigston. This is 2556 (SHE 556S) in Belgrave Gate on 18 August, showing off its gleaming new paint job.

Several Daimler Fleetlines moved across to the Wreake Valley fleet in the early 1990s. One example, 2772, only had its front repainted, but 2763 (GHM 763N) received the full works. Unusually, it was employed on County Hall Park & Ride work in this High Street scene, but after only a year, it was withdrawn in September 1991 and used for spares.

Midland Fox next acquired **Blands of Stamford** in July 1990. Their fleet of coaches included DAF MB200s and an SB3000, Bova and TAZ3200 integrals, three Scania K112s and a Mercedes 811D. This is one of four Bedford YMTs, 60 (RBC 500W), in Blands livery but with Fairtax fleetnames, photographed between duties in the coach park in Peterborough in early 1991. Within months it would join the training fleet, where, renumbered 9047, it notched up a further eleven years.

Above and below: One of the Leyland Leopards joining the fleet from Barton Buses earlier in 1990, 370 (RVO 670L) was given Blands livery and was loading for Stamford at Queensgate bus station, Peterborough, in September, while former Blands DAF MB200, 153 (OWA 23X), was seen at the Burton Street garage in 1993 after a repaint into red Fairtax livery. It would move to Hinckley, and then to Stamford, before withdrawal in 2000.

Six Ivecos joined the fleet from Bee Line, Manchester, in August 1990. Northern Counties-bodied M258 (E188 CNE) was the oldest, although it was still two months short of its second birthday. Newly painted into Fox Cub livery, it was bound for Rowley Fields, a suburb in the south of Leicester, when photographed in Humberstone Gate.

M246 (H246 MOE) was the middle one of three new Carlyle-bodied Ivecos acquired in October 1990 and based at Sandacre Street until 1995/96. It was returning from Derby when seen in Gravel Street on 7 August 1993; four years earlier this would have been an LC&B duty for a Leyland National.

After working for two National Travel divisions and Ribble, Plaxton-bodied Leyland Leopard 475 (SFV 207P) came to Midland Fox in September 1984. In 1989/90 it had a spell with Wreake Valley as its No. 3, which was probably nearing its end as the livery seems to be in a state of transition. It was pictured in Humberstone Gate outside the C&A store, which closed in 2001, a decade after 475 was withdrawn and used for spares.

Midland Fox had acquired the business of **NWP Travel**, Hinckley, in April 1990. Nine months later, TGM acquired Hills of Nuneaton trading as **V & M Hills**, at which point NWP Travel was merged with it and the name dropped. The Hills business brought with it a Leyland Royal Tiger/Roe Doyen coach, which became 13 (A936 MRW, DJI 1333, A919 LJC, 429 UFM). Having transferred to Wigston and donned Foxhound livery, it was seen on a quiet Sunday in February 1994 outside Leicester London Road station whilst on rail replacement duty.

New to Pilgrim Coaches, Leyland Doyen-bodied Royal Tiger passed to V & M Hills in 1991, moving to Midland Fox as its 30 (C69 BFX) in October 1992. On 26 June 1993, it was seen in Church Square North, Market Harborough, with a party of morris dancers. Sold in 1994, four owners later, it was destroyed by fire in Glasgow in June 2007.

Three Leyland Leopards included in the purchase of V & M Hills crossed to the Midland Fox fleet in April 1993. The photo of 317 (TVC 402W, DJI 8467, PWK 5W) in the Jacknall Road outstation yard, Hinckley, on 11 June 1994 also features some withdrawn Ford Transits, M133, M132 and M57 being those nearest the camera.

When London Buses began to dispose of its RH class of Carlyle-bodied Ivecos, Midland Fox stepped in to obtain five, which became M248–52. The last of these, M252 (C512 DYM), went to the LC&B operation and received advertising livery for children's store Kiddysway. It was on its way back to Leicester when photographed at the Beaumont Leys Centre in 1993.

September 1991 saw the arrival of Freight Rover Sherpas M458/59 from fellow Drawlane group member North Western. M458 (D58 TLV) was always based at Hinckley, and was seen in the town's old bus station in 1993 with a plethora of notices about the 700 service and the special fares available. It passed to Southern National in 1995.

Daimler Fleetlines with Park Royal bodywork that have not been illustrated yet are those which passed to London Country in 1980 for driver training. They came to Midland Fox in 1982 and were shared between Wigston, Coalville and Swadlincote. By February 1991, 2654 (MLK 654L) was a Southgate Street bus, and in snowy conditions, it was entering St Margaret's prior to a run out to Shepshed. Two months later it was withdrawn and used to keep other members of the fleet going.

Five more ex-South Yorkshire PTE Metrobuses came via Stevensons in December 1991 and January 1992, and much was made of them having Rolls-Royce Eagle engines. Three years later and although 2477 (JHE 177W) is working a Saturday Oadby service from a temporary terminus in Charles Street during rebuilding on the site of the former Lewis's store, a clue to its weekday occupation is provided by the livery.

The Bristol VR3 allocated to Melton Mowbray that was pictured earlier transferred to the Fen Travel operation in June 1992 and was replaced by Leyland Fleetline Park Royal 2933 (OJD 133R), which had come from Stevensons. It was photographed at the Burton Street garage in 1993, alongside Fairtax recovery vehicle SUP 402M.

Former Midland Red Leyland National 2s 3809/12 were received from North Western, who had had them from Midland Red North, in May 1991. They were allocated to Loughborough, though in Midland Fox livery, and 3809 (BVP 809V) was seen in The Rushes on a town service later in the year. Both vehicles were transferred to Colchester in 1994.

Six Renault S56/Northern Counties arrived from South Yorkshire Transport in February 1992 for Fairtax work. They received a brighter livery than the Transits and were all named – M465 (D135 OWG) was *The Forrester*. It was found in John Street, Oakham, working the 'Rutland Flyer' service from Melton Mowbray to Corby on 6 March 1993. All six were withdrawn in 1997.

National Welsh went into receivership in early 1992 and Leyland Nationals that passed to Midland Fox have already been illustrated. Four Freight Rover Sherpas, M467/69–71, were also taken. M471 (G266 GKG) was spotted in Gravel Street on the former Astill & Jordan 94 in November 1992. After withdrawal in 1995 it was another that saw further service with Southern National.

New to Alexander (Midland), then to Kelvin, MCW Metrobus 2489 (CKS 389X) came to Southgate Street from North Western in July 1992 and appears to have had no preparatory work carried out in readiness for its new career, apart from the fleetname on the front panel. It was seen in London Road, Oadby, on 31 July, and, in fairness, was repainted into fleet livery soon after.

The south Leicestershire village of Cosby has suffered from flooding on many occasions, not least in 1993 when 2964 (OJD 414R) splashed through it en route to Broughton Astley. Midland Fox took twenty-nine of these Park Royal-bodied Leyland Fleetline B20s from London Buses in the summer of 1992 and apart from 2980, which was only used for spares, the rest were withdrawn by the end of 1994.

The arrival of the B20s presaged a steady withdrawal of the remaining Daimler Fleetlines. The last to go was one of the oldest, 2700 (TGX 707M), withdrawn in early 1996 after twelve years with Midland Fox. At the time of this December 1992 photo, it had just moved garages from Southgate Street to Wigston, and was loading in Charles Street for a run to its new base on the 48.

A new competitor appeared in 1992 in the shape of Countesthorpe-based Deeward Travel. Midland Fox joined in combat with two B20 Fleetlines: 2941, which retained London livery, and 2994 (OJD 394R), in all-over red. A board in the windscreen claimed it was on loan to 'Red Bus'. This Charles Street photo on 30 March 1993 also shows a Deeward Bristol LH and Ford Transit M92, also part of the ultimately successful Midland Fox response.

North Western provided six L608Ds, the first of the type for Midland Fox, in August 1992. This was the only Reeves Burgess-bodied example (the others were by Alexander) and all were allocated to Coalville. M299 (D209 SKD) was resting between duties in St Margaret's in 1993; when its service days were over it became maintenance van X951.

Newer, though nonetheless second-hand Leyland Olympian/Northern Counties double-deckers came to Wigston garage from Kentish Bus in September 1992. They received fleet numbers 4529–33, and this is 4529 (G506 SFT) leaving St Margaret's for Countesthorpe on the 27th, bringing another new livery to Leicester's streets. In 1999, they were part of the transfer to Arriva North West, along with 4521–25.

Midland Fox had two Alexander-bodied Leyland Leopards, 9056/57, from Bluebird Northern and Stagecoach Perth respectively, for driver training in August 1992. The livery of red with a black skirt suited 9056 (OSJ 630R), which was seen in Southgates on 26 October 1992. Sadly, it was stolen in June 1993 and never recovered.

Wallace Arnold coaches were popular with many operators when it came to sourcing well-maintained and still-youthful vehicles. Midland Fox took two such Volvo B10Ms, 236/37, in October 1992. Loading for a National Express service to London in Gravel Street on 7 November 1992, 236 (F406 DUG) became a training vehicle at the end of 2001.

Sunday 28 March 1993, 7.45 a.m., and the Year 9s at Kibworth High School are assembling for a field trip to Northumberland, the author's son amongst them. Transport was provided by Leyland Royal Tiger 13, Leyland Tiger 29 and DAF MB200/Plaxton 8006 (LJI 5631, B568 NJF), which had joined Midland Fox from Welsh, Upton, near Pontefract, in May 1988.

Last seen in these pages in Eastbourne, 8007 (LJI 5632, B196 PAY) now appears in Exhibition Road, London SW7, on 19 June 1992, having transferred to the Shelton Orsborn fleet, whose livery it carries. This was some four months after the Shelton Orsborn garage and operations were sold by way of a management buyout, the new company trading as L & B Travel. Midland Fox retained the Shelton Orsborn name.

Fen Travel took to the streets of Peterborough in July 1992 to take on the incumbent operator, Viscount – part of Cambus Holdings. Based at what was the Midland Fox and former Blands garage at Ryhall, near Stamford, vehicles included several transferred from the Midland Fox fleet, such as Leopard 367 (RVO 667L), picking up a healthy load for Stamford at Queensgate bus station. This bus war lasted until February 1993, when Fen Travel went into liquidation.

Most of the vehicles that passed from Midland Fox to Fen Travel came back again after hostilities ceased – as did the premises at Ryhall. Back at Melton Mowbray garage, 612 (796 UHT, NMV 612W) displayed Foxhound fleetnames on its Fen Travel livery when seen on 3 November 1993.

Fen Travel had picked up five Freight Rover Sherpas from the sale of National Welsh assets which went on to join Midland Fox. They had relatively short lives, being withdrawn between October 1995 and May 1996. M430 (D70 OKG) was seen outside the Sainsbury's store at Grove Park on 11 June 1994.

An unusual occurrence was recorded on 3 April 1993, when the entire bus station area at St Margaret's was closed temporarily due to a suspected gas leak. Two Leylands, Fleetline 2541 (SHE 541S) and, in the background, Olympian 4490, were obliged to load for their next journeys in Burleys Way.

The British Bus and Cowie Group Years

The first purchases following the renaming of Drawlane to British Bus were five Merseybus ECW-bodied Leyland Olympians in March 1993, assigned to Southgate Street. Photographed while negotiating the roundabout at the Charles Street/Belgrave Gate junction the following month, 4488 (ACM 710X) still bears its Merseybus blind display, which, being non-standard, was soon replaced.

Four Renault S56/Northern Counties vehicles were acquired from Stagecoach in Hants and Surrey, new owners of Alder Valley, in August 1993. At least one operated in the attractive two-tone green and yellow livery before all were given different advertising liveries for British Telecom. M415 (E415 EPE) was returning to the centre from South Knighton on the 27A when seen on Queens Road a month after arrival.

Three further MCW Metrobuses with Scottish origins and the less usual Alexander bodywork appeared in 1993. They had been destined for Bee Line, Manchester, but were rerouted to assist Midland Fox in the latest bus war. One of the services Midland Fox registered against an existing LCB route was the 825 to Beaumont Leys, on which 2481 (CKS 391X) was found on 22 September.

The people of Evington were very lucky to have a coach such as Leyland Tiger/Duple 27 (B151 ALG) to ride on for the few months that the bus war took place. It was one of four received from Crosville that were repainted and sent to Wigston and was on the 822 to Evington, mirroring the LCB 22 and seen in Charles Street, also on 22 September 1993.

Midland Fox did well out of Leyland Leopard 719 (AFJ 719T), which came from Devon General in August 1983. By 1993, now based at Coalville, it had a role to play in the bus war. LCB operated a number of services from its Barlestone garage acquired with the Gibsons business in 1979. Midland Fox registered the Ibstock route to compete with LCBs 152/53 services, and 719 was getting ahead of the LCB Dennis Dominator in this High Street photo from October. Note the short-lived dual-purpose livery with bold yellow stripes and large fleetnames and logos.

This is 3744 (UHG 744R), one of two seventeen-year-old Leyland Nationals received from Ribble in September 1993 (along with 3709), operating in a Midland Fox and Ribble hybrid livery. Both were destined to become Greenway rebuilds, ending up at London & Country's Guildford & West Surrey division. The photo was taken at St Margaret's on 16 October 1993.

Six Alexander-bodied Scania N113DRBs, 4153–58, came to Midland Fox after BTS of Borehamwood lost the London contract work on which they had been employed. They were allocated to Southgate Street in November 1993 and working a 114 Ratby and Groby circular, 4153 (F153 DET) was leaving St Margaret's just days afterwards.

In the same month, three Leyland Olympians with East Lancs bodywork new to Southampton, 4482–84, were taken into stock, their previous owner being the ill-fated Sheffield Omnibus. Allocated to Wigston, 4483 (A280 ROW) was seen as it made the turn into Charles Street on an X61 working in 1994; by now Midland Fox only worked the Leicester to Market Harborough section.

Above and below: Midland Fox had four Robin Hood-bodied Ivecos on loan from a dealer in February 1993. Two were from United Counties, including 44 (D44 DNH), which didn't carry a fleet number or stay long with the company. Also illustrated is 614 (D614 BCK), one of two new to Ribble, and after the February loan, it returned to Sandacre Street from September to December. Both photos were taken in Gravel Street.

And when your time is up ... Willowbrook-bodied Leyland Leopard 842 (LOA 842X) was withdrawn in April 1993 and was used for spares starting in the following August. The process was still ongoing when it was photographed in Coalville garage in November.

Quality second-hand purchases in January 1994 were of Leyland Olympians 4480/81 from Colchester. The photo was taken on the 20th, and it appears that 4480 (C42 HHJ) had only very recently entered service. It spent the next six years at Wigston, two more at Stamford and was sold to Silverdale, Nottingham, along with 4481 in 2002.

New in 1994, with deliveries beginning in January, were twenty Alexander-bodied Mercedes 709Ds. M305/06 went to Coalville to work the East Midlands Airport car park shuttles, for which they had a suitable livery, if not blind display. M306 (L306 AUT) had just returned to the terminal building on 9 September 1995, with former Stevensons M330 on the 122 Derby service at the rear.

The Marks & Spencer shuttle services were originally in the hands of Ivecos M239/40. They were replaced by two of the new 709Ds, M315 (L315 AUT), seen in Market Harborough High Street on 1 April 1994, and M319. They would be superseded in turn by a couple of Dennis Dart SLFs, 2207/08, which seated thirty-nine as opposed to twenty-five in the 709Ds, in 1999.

Two ECW-bodied Leyland Olympians were acquired in April 1994 from Reading. Preparing to turn into Charles Street from Humberstone Gate, coach-seated 4479 (D81 UTF) would have provided a comfortable ride on the long journey from Nuneaton. Once again work on the former Lewis's site is in view, this time to preserve the famous tower. Humberstone Gate, so long a departure point for Leicester buses, was pedestrianised in 1999.

Seven more Ivecos came south in May and August 1994. New to Amberline of Liverpool, they were with North Western prior to the transfer. M265 (G249 GCC) was immediately given overall advertising for Mc-in-Tyres and spent four years in Leicester, working out of Sandacre Street and, later, Thurmaston.

Six further 709Ds that appeared in June 1994 had Leicester Coach Builders bodywork, a first for Midland Fox, and took fleet numbers M323–28. The last three transferred to Luton & District after just five months. The type was easily identifiable by the box-like destination displays. M325 (L325 AUT) was on the 27 Pendlebury Drive stand in Charles Street in October 1994.

Also in June 1994, Crosville Cymru provided ten more Iveco/Robin Hoods of 1988 vintage, which took fleet numbers M259/67–75. M274 (F274 CEY) was repainted and allocated to Market Harborough; on 4 October 1994 it was waiting time at the temporary terminus for the Great Bowden service in Adam and Eve Street.

The idea of the Greenway project was that East Lancs coach builders would rebuild mid-life Leyland Nationals and thus extend their service lives. Midland Fox put ten into service in the summer of 1994, 2156–65, seven of which had been in the fleet previously. Displaying the aesthetically pleasing East Lancs body, 2158 (JIL 2158), the former 3649, was motoring along Coventry Road, Hinckley, on 11 June.

Not the most attractive bus Midland Fox ever operated, Mercedes 811D/Robin Hood M402 (F272 OPX) was new to R & I, London, and came to Leicester from Stevensons in September 1994. After a year in the city it was farmed out to Hinckley, then to Coalville, for whom it was working when this photo in Market Street, Ashby de la Zouch, was taken.

'Fox Cabs' were launched in September 1994 with a fleet of twenty Carbodies taxis in plain red livery. This was no great surprise given that Derby, with which Midland Fox was closely associated, had had a taxi fleet since 1990. In time, however, the business didn't fit with Arriva's plans and was sold to Swifts in September 2000. Not easy to photograph in traffic, CO16 (M916 DHP) was empty when found in Sandacre Street on 21 December 1994 – problem solved.

In October 1994, Midland Fox received its first new double-deckers for five years, British Bus investing in twenty of these handsome Scania N113s with Alexander bodywork. Thirteen were allocated to Wigston, seven to Southgate Street. Seen in Charles Street when new, 4159 (M159 GRY) was passing the site of the Haymarket bus station, still under construction at that time.

The last of the former South Yorkshire PTE Metrobuses to find their way to Midland Fox from Stevensons were 2493/94. Taking its place on the 29 stand in Belgrave Gate on 1 October 1994, 2494 (JWF 494W) still carried its former operator's livery. It did eventually visit the paint shop, and remained at Southgate Street until July 1998.

Two Ford Transits, M119 and M128, were given special liveries for the Leicester Market Shuttle, which began on 31 May 1994, an initiative paid for by the market traders themselves. The photo of M119 (C519 TJF) was taken in Market Place South on 3 June; unfortunately the venture wasn't successful and ended after just a few months.

The last five N113s were received over the three months up to February 1995. In glorious sunshine on 6 July that year, the last of the batch, 4178 (M178 GRY), was leaving St Margaret's, fully loaded, on the seasonal X11 for Warwick and Stratford. It was transferred to Arriva Midlands North at Cannock in May 2007.

New to Pathfinder (Newark) in 1992 with fleet number 20, this Dormobile-bodied Mercedes 709D came to Midland Fox as its M543 (K543 OGA) for four months in May 1995 before moving on to Luton & District. It was photographed in Gravel Street on 6 July.

A surprising acquisition in September 1995, Leyland Leopard/Alexander 388 (YCS 92T) came from Maidstone & District but started life at Western SMT seventeen years previously. It spent a year at Wigston, and was on the Charles Street 80 stand on 21 September 1996, two months before it was withdrawn and sold to a dealer.

Two former Kentish Bus Scania N112DRB/Alexanders, 4151/52, were allocated to Wigston in December 1995. It seemed that 4151 (E701 XKR) was mainly confined to schools services until it received fleet livery, and in this 7 February 1996 view, it has just emerged from the depths of Station Street garage ready to work a service from the Robert Smyth School in Market Harborough. In July 2001, 4151 was sold to an Irish operator, 4152 to Black Prince.

Some demonstrators used by Midland Fox didn't stay long, and to get a photo of one could be quite an accomplishment. Dennis Lance/Optare Sigma M21 UUA was working a Sunday roster on 21 May 1995 when it was found in Hunters Way, Oadby, on the 31. It later went to Tees, and was operated by Felix of Stanley, Derbyshire, between 1995 and 2000.

It's March 1995 and Leyland Tiger 28 (BPR 108Y) is still earning its keep on long-distance services such as the X66. Photographed alongside West Midlands Buses Leyland Lynx 1172, it has just left the Bull Ring bus station in Birmingham for the journey back to Leicester. It continued in service, albeit relegated to the Stamford garage, until 1999.

The Haymarket Theatre commissioned overall advertisements for its productions for several years in the mid-1990s. This is Leyland Olympian 4508 (A508 EJF), seen in Belgrave Gate in September 1993, by which time it had received non-standard, if conventional, blinds in place of the original dot matrix, and a splendid design for *Rock of Ages*. It was conveniently parked outside the venue at the time.

The first in a series of advertisements for Leicester City Council's Road Safety Campaign appeared in 1993. There were several variations, some humorous ('Leicestershire drivers do not travel too fast … pigs might fly'), some serious, such as this example carried by Leyland Olympian 4530 (G508 SFT) during 1995, seen in the Haymarket bus station. The extension of the 37 to Mowmacre Hill ran in competition with Leicester CityBus for a time.

Midland Fox had run well-patronised Park & Ride services to the city centre from County Hall via the A50 and Leicester Racecourse via the A6 since 1992. In 1995 only, a third site was used, the Sears British Shoe factory on Sunningdale Road via the A47. It operated as the 103 on four Saturdays prior to Christmas. In advertising livery for The Shires shopping centre, Leyland Olympian 4511 (A511 EJF) stands in High Street on 9 December.

Fifteen more Mercedes 709Ds were received between September 1995 and February 1996. The penultimate member of the batch, M357 (N357 OBC), became the designated vehicle for a new service, the X26 'Mountsorrel Flyer', which started on 24 February 1997 and took a faster route out of Leicester than the existing 126/127. It was seen in High Street in March 1997, displaying an unfortunate misspelling of the destination on the blind.

After a career of twenty-two years with United Counties and Luton & District, Leyland National 2155 (GNV 656N) came to Midland Fox in February 1996. Seen in a busy High Street that same month on the main Leicester–Nuneaton 158 service, it would remain at Hinckley until withdrawal in 2000.

A new livery and brand made their debut on fourteen East Lancs-bodied Scania L113s, the first seven of which entered service on 4 March 1996. Southgate Street took 2166–75, while 2176–79 went to Thurmaston, where they were used on the X1 Melton Mowbray service. When seen in Narborough on the first day, Urban Fox 2172 (N172 PUT) was on its way back to Leicester.

The four Thurmaston-based vehicles carried County Fox fleetnames on the dark blue livery. Loading in the Haymarket bus station on 12 May 1996, 2179 (N179 PUT) was bound for Melton.

One of two Volvo B10Ms acquired in May 1996, 212 (N212 TBC) was photographed on the National Express stand at St Margaret's in November 1996. It was re-registered 662 NKR in 2000, though after temporary withdrawal following an accident in 2002, that passed to sister coach 211.

Midland Fox won the contract for the Kettering station to Corby town centre rail link service in 1995. Mercedes 709Ds M344/45 were used until Plaxton-bodied M359/60 arrived in September 1996. These were given an appropriate livery, that of franchise holder Midland Mainline, operated by National Express. M359 (P111 MML) was seen at Kettering station on 14 June 1997. The pair were replaced by Dennis Dart SLFs in 2003.

October and November 1996 saw the arrival of thirteen new Volvo Olympians for Wigston, all receiving Urban Fox livery on Northern Counties bodywork. The Cowie Group had taken over British Bus in August 1996, but it's likely that these were on order before that date, which would make them the last true Midland Fox acquisitions. 4602 (P602 CAY) was on a 48 working in Bull Head Street, Wigston, on 28 March 1997.

The Shires acquired this Dennis Javelin/Duple coach, 136 (IIL 4580), from Rochester & Marshall in 1994. Two years later it was on a short loan to Midland Fox at Market Harborough, where it was spotted in the Springfield Street garage yard on 26 April. The blind is set to 'SCHOOL', which is likely to have been the full extent of its duties whilst here. The garage was subsequently sold and the site repurposed as an Aldi supermarket.

Seventeen Northern Counties-bodied Dodge S56s joined the fleet from Derby City Transport between October 1996 and February 1997. M470–81 were new to either South Yorkshire or Cleveland Transit, while the others, M485–89, were from United. On 24 May 1997, Hinckley's M480 (E330 LHN) was pictured in The Borough en route to the 82 Barwell stand in Regent Street. All were withdrawn by December 1997.

May 1997 saw the arrival of a pair of Mercedes L609Ds from Maidstone & District. It was no surprise to see M281 (E61 UKL) operating in its former owner's colours when spotted in The Green, Great Bowden, on the 17th. What was more surprising was that both it and M282 were repainted into the blue 'Urban' livery, which up until that point had been intended for new vehicles only.

The new Mercedes O814Ds that took fleet numbers M101–26 vacated by the Ford Transits, appearing from May to July 1997, were received in 'Urban' livery, although they retained Fox Cub fleetnames. M104 (P104 HCH) was bound for Rowley Fields in this July 1997 photo. The O814D was now the new standard midibus; by June 1998 a further forty-four, M127–70, were in service.

The next batch of O814Ds, M127–46, had bodywork by Plaxton instead of Alexander, appearing in November and December 1997. Midland Fox hired in a Plaxton-bodied demonstrator, 296 (P296 JHE), from July until the first of the main order arrived. It was seen in High Street about to work the eastern section of the 52 to Scraptoft.

Leicester's first purpose-built Park & Ride site at Meynells Gorse, Leicester Forest East, opened on 4 August 1997. Midland Fox won the contract and put four new thirty-nine-seat Plaxton-bodied Dennis Dart SLFs in 'Quicksilver Shuttle' livery on the route, which was numbered 103. On the first day, 2203 (P203 HRY) was awaiting mid-morning custom.

Although it had disposed of its Leyland National 2s some years previously, Midland Fox took two back into stock in August 1997. The former Midland Red 813 and 831 were renumbered 2153/54; the latter worked out of Coalville for two years, while 2153 (BVP 813V) was based at Thurmaston, painted in County Fox blue livery, and, as here in the Haymarket bus station, could often be seen helping out on Melton Mowbray services.

In November 1997 the Cowie Group adopted a new name – Arriva plc. That same month, two Volvo B10M coaches were transferred in from Luton & District, becoming 234/35, heralding the introduction of a nationwide livery of aquamarine and stone. As yet without fleetnames, 234 (HIL 7594, E662 UNE) was loading for Leicester in The Square, Kibworth Beauchamp, on 29 December 1997.

It might be gone, but it hasn't been forgotten. One of Arriva Midlands' fleet of Wrightbus-bodied VDL DB250s, 4752 (FJ06 ZSX), was given the memorable yellow and red livery to mark the thirty-fifth anniversary of Midland Fox, with the message 'Proud of our heritage – Proud of our future' emblazoned between decks. It was seen on Hinckley Road, Leicester Forest East, on its way to Market Bosworth, on 4 March 2019.